OBAMA

The ... on of Ame ... sident

by Agni... itu Hayden

Consultant:
Dr. Phil Schoenberg
Professor of American History and Government
Vaughn College of Aeronautics and Technology
Flushing, New York

CAPSTONE PRESS
a capstone imprint

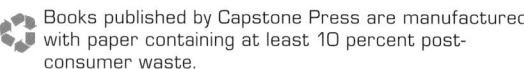 is published by Capstone Press,
1710 Roe Crest Drive
North Mankato, Minnesota 56003.

www.capstonepub.com

Books published by Capstone Press are manufactured with paper containing at least 10 percent post-consumer waste.

Library of Congress Cataloging-in-Publication Data
Biskup, Agnieszka.
Obama : the historic election of America's 44th president / by Agnieszka Biskup; illustrated by Seitu Hayden.
    p. cm.—(Graphic library. American graphic)
Includes bibliographical references and index.
    Summary: "In graphic novel format, follows President Barack Obama during the 2008 presidential election campaign"—Provided by publisher.
ISBN 978-1-4296-6016-7 (library binding)
ISBN 978-1-4296-7339-6 (paperback)

1. Presidents—United States—Election—2008—Juvenile literature. 2. Obama, Barack—Juvenile literature. 3. Presidential candidates—United States—Biography—Juvenile literature. 4. Presidents—United States—Biography—Juvenile literature. I. Hayden, Seitu. II. Title. III. Series.

E906.B57 2012
324.973'0905—dc22

                                2011009923

Photo Credits:
Official White House photo by Pete Souza, 28–29

Direct quotations appear in yellow on the following pages:

Page 4 from *The Audacity of Hope: Thoughts on Reclaiming the American Dream*, Barack Obama (New York: Crown Publishers, 2006).

Page 5–6 from "Keynote Address at the 2004 Democratic National Convention," *The Washington Post*, July 27, 2004.

Page 8 from *The Bridge: The Life and Rise of Barack Obama*, David Remnick (New York: Alfred A. Knopf, 2010).

Page 10, 15, and 17 from *Obama: The Historic Journey*, Jill Abramson (New York: Callaway, 2009).

Page 11 from "Senator Barack Obama's Announcement for President," *The New York Times*, February 10, 2007.

Page 19 from "Clinton's Concession Speech," *The New York Times*, June 7, 2008.

Page 21 from *Obama: The Historic Front Pages*, David Elliot Cohen and Mark Greenberg (New York: Sterling, 2009).

Page 23, from "McCain: Fundamentals of Economy are 'Strong' but 'Threatened'." *The Washington Post*, September 15, 2008.

Page 26 (second panel) from "McCain's Concession Speech" *The New York Times*, November 5, 2008.

Page 26 (bottom) and 27, from "Obama's Grant Park Speech," *The New York Times*, November 5, 2008.

Art Director: Nathan Gassman

Editor: Lori Shores

Media Researcher: Wanda Winch

Production Specialist: Eric Manske

Printed in the United States of America in Stevens Point, Wisconsin.
112012   007015R

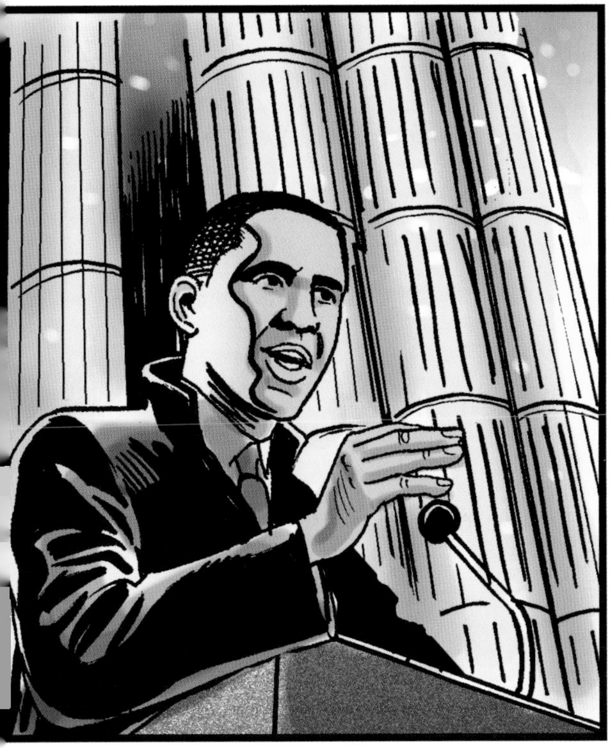

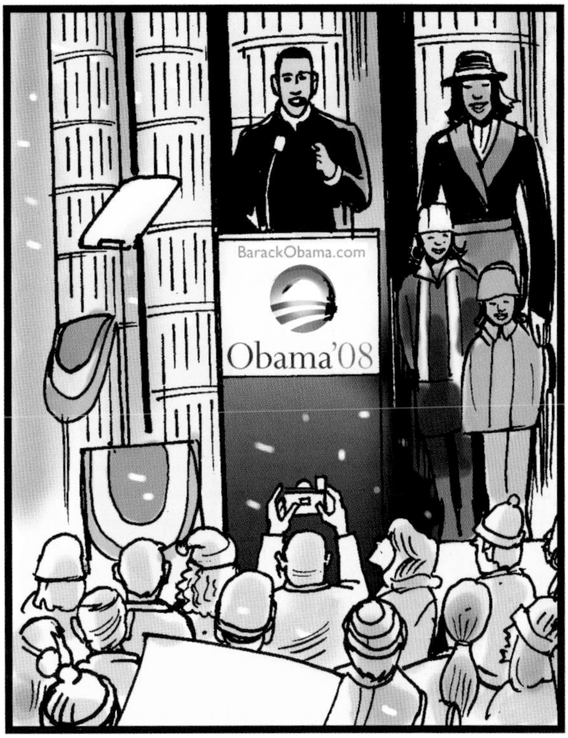
BarackObama.com
Obama'08

In 2004 Democrats from around the country gathered in Boston. They met to officially nominate Senator John Kerry as their candidate for president.

Kerry had chosen Illinois Democrat Barack Obama to give the keynote speech at the convention. Obama was running for the United States Senate, but he was barely known outside Illinois. Tonight, he would be placed in the national spotlight.

Obama and his wife, Michelle, waited backstage. Obama was feeling a bit nervous.

My stomach is feeling grumbly.

Just don't screw it up, buddy!

On that July night, Obama introduced himself to America.

Tonight is a particular honor for me because, let's face it,

my presence on this stage is pretty unlikely.

My father was a foreign student, born and raised in a small village in Kenya.

He grew up herding goats, went to school in a tin-roof shack.

While studying here, my father met my mother. She was born in a town on the other side of the world, in Kansas.

They would give me an African name, Barack, or "blessed," believing that in a tolerant America, your name is no barrier to success.

I stand here knowing that my story is part of the larger American story ... that in no other country on Earth is my story even possible.

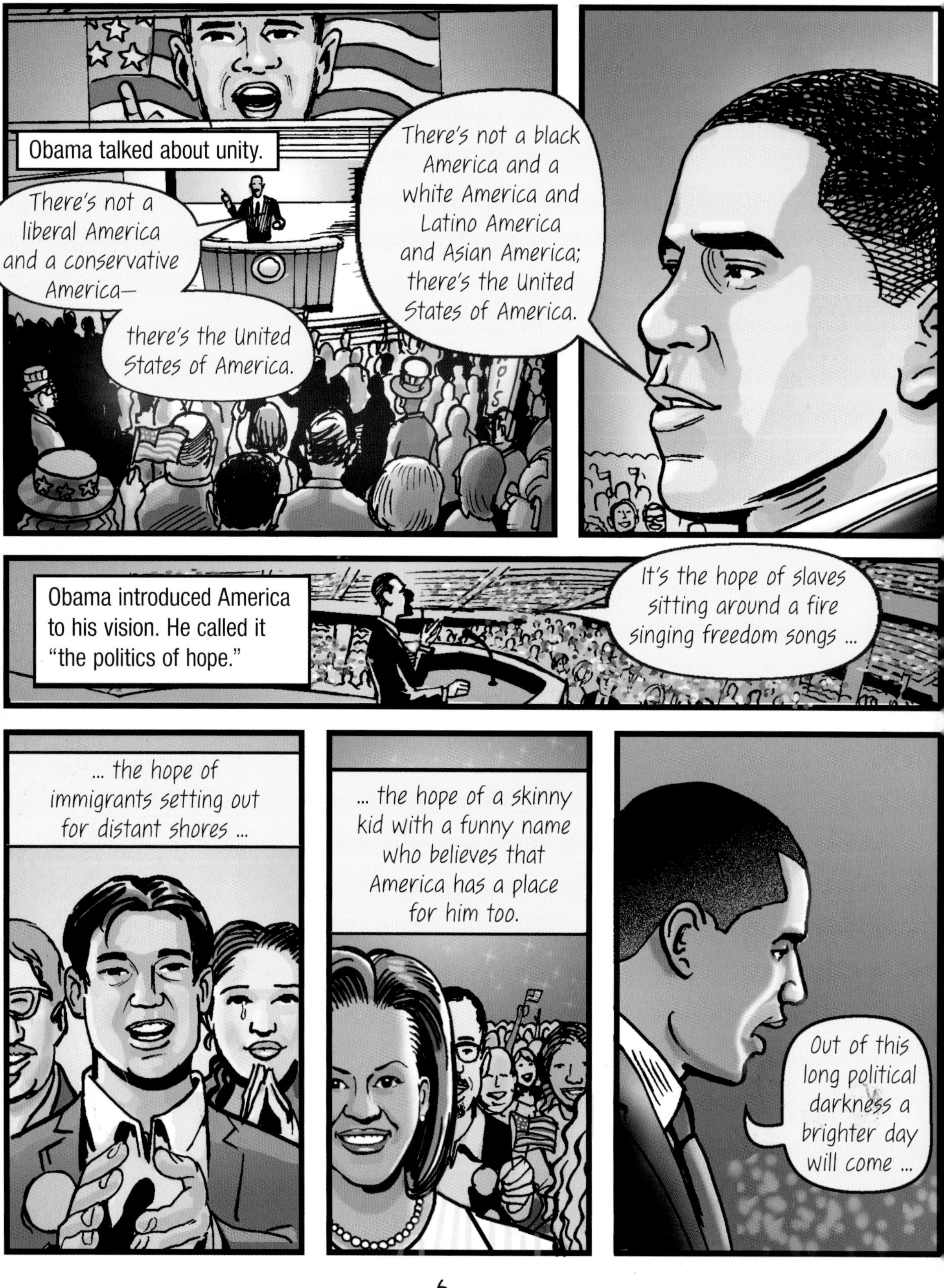
Obama talked about unity.
There's not a liberal America and a conservative America—
there's the United States of America.
There's not a black America and a white America and Latino America and Asian America; there's the United States of America.
Obama introduced America to his vision. He called it "the politics of hope."
It's the hope of slaves sitting around a fire singing freedom songs ...
... the hope of immigrants setting out for distant shores ...
... the hope of a skinny kid with a funny name who believes that America has a place for him too.
Out of this long political darkness a brighter day will come ...

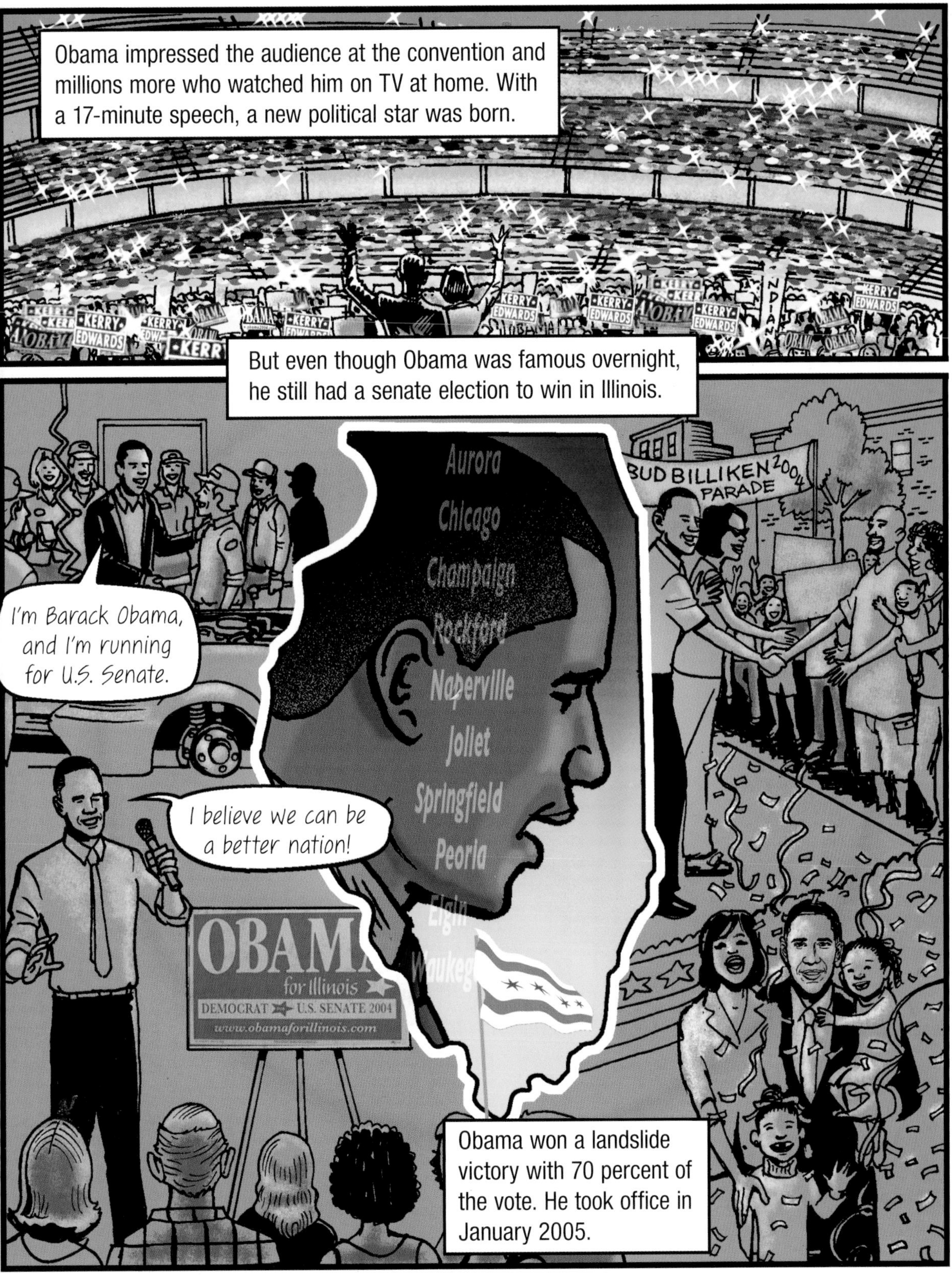
Obama impressed the audience at the convention and millions more who watched him on TV at home. With a 17-minute speech, a new political star was born.
KERRY EDWARDS
OBAMA
INDIANA
But even though Obama was famous overnight, he still had a senate election to win in Illinois.
I'm Barack Obama, and I'm running for U.S. Senate.
Aurora
Chicago
Champaign
Rockford
Naperville
Joliet
Springfield
Peoria
Elgin
BUD BILLIKEN 2004 PARADE
I believe we can be a better nation!
OBAMA for Illinois
DEMOCRAT U.S. SENATE 2004
www.obamaforillinois.com
Obama won a landslide victory with 70 percent of the vote. He took office in January 2005.

Obama had only just been elected senator, but people were already asking if he'd run for president.

Are you going to run for president?

I was elected yesterday.

The notion that somehow I'm going to start running for higher office, it doesn't make sense.

His daughter Malia was interested too.

Are you going to try to be president? Shouldn't you be vice president first?

After the election, Obama moved to Washington D.C. He got to work in the senate helping to create new legislation.

Obama missed his family. He and Michelle had decided not to move the family to Washington. He returned home to Chicago when he could.

Goodnight, Sasha.

Goodnight, Malia.

Obama's second book, *The Audacity of Hope*, was published in 2006. The book became a bestseller, making him even more widely known. Reporters and camera crews trailed him. He appeared on the covers of national magazines.

Obama traveled all over the country, signing books and giving speeches to support other Democratic candidates. His appearances always drew crowds.

People were drawn to Obama and his ideas of hope and change.

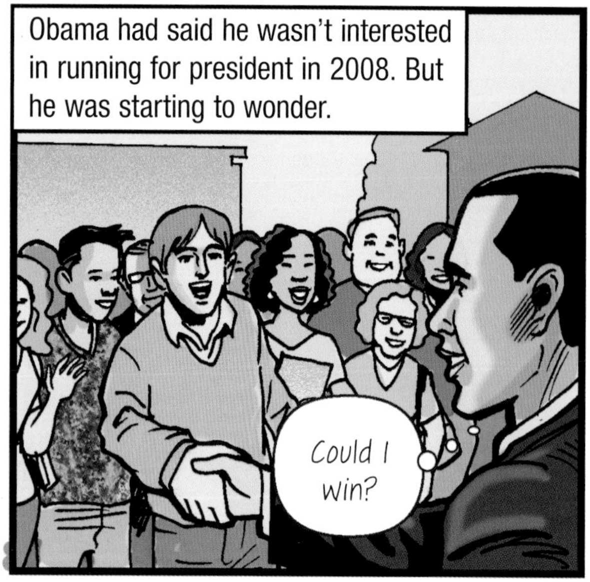
Obama had said he wasn't interested in running for president in 2008. But he was starting to wonder.
Could I win?

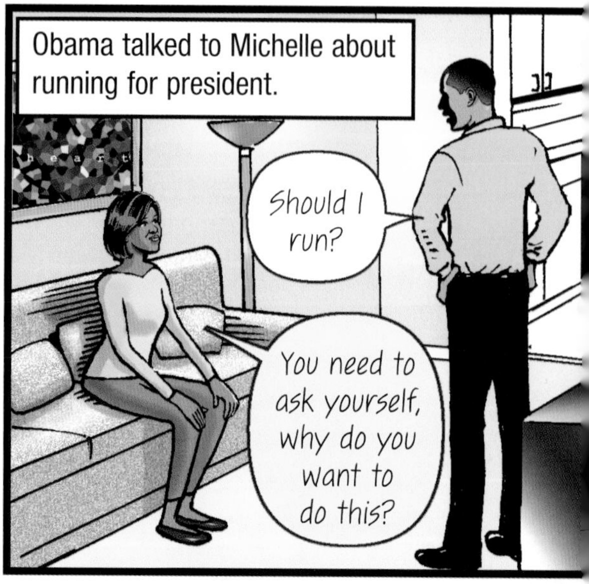
Obama talked to Michelle about running for president.
Should I run?
You need to ask yourself, why do you want to do this?

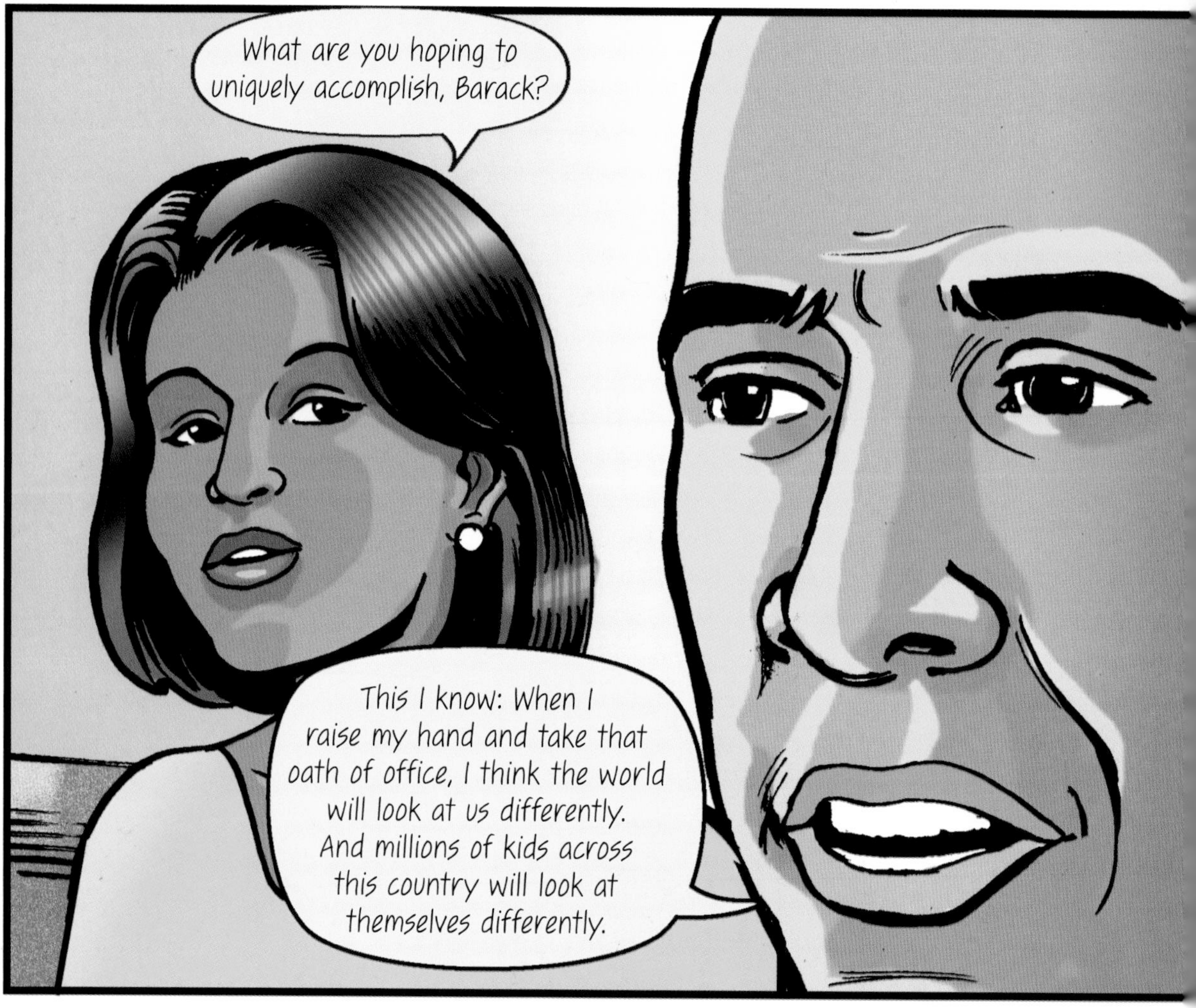
What are you hoping to uniquely accomplish, Barack?
This I know: When I raise my hand and take that oath of office, I think the world will look at us differently. And millions of kids across this country will look at themselves differently.

February 10, 2007

Obama made his declaration in front of the Old State Capitol in Springfield, Illinois. The location was also where Abraham Lincoln, one of Obama's personal heroes, began his political career.

BarackObama.com

Obama'08

I stand before you today to announce my candidacy for President of the United States of America.

Again, he called for change.

I know I haven't spent a lot of time learning the ways of Washington. But I've been there long enough to know that the ways of Washington must change.

Each and every time, a new generation has risen up and done what's needed to be done. Today we are called once more ...

... and it is time for our generation to answer that call.

CHAPTER 2

The Democratic Nomination

Obama wasn't the only candidate seeking the Democratic Party nomination for president. His rivals included many prominent Democrats.

New York senator and former first lady Hillary Rodham Clinton was considered the front-runner in the race.

The other candidates believed that Obama didn't have enough political experience to run for president and win. In national polls, he trailed Clinton by more than 20 percentage points.

But they underestimated Obama's appeal to voters and his determination to win.

He set a grueling pace. Obama rose at dawn to talk to factory workers before their shifts started.

He met with voters throughout the day.

At night, he attended dinners and gave more speeches.

With his message of change, Obama attracted many young supporters who worked tirelessly on his behalf.

He quickly built an organization of volunteers across the country.

Obama used the Internet to generate enthusiasm and get donations for his campaign. He took in millions of dollars in small contributions from people all over the country, raising record sums.

January 3, 2008

Only one candidate from each party can be chosen to run for president. Members of the party select the candidate by voting in primary elections held in many states.

Obama's savvy campaigning made him a surprise winner in the Iowa caucus. Clinton placed third.

January 8, 2008

Clinton won in New Hampshire!

In the next key test, Obama was disappointed by the primary election results.

I guess this is going to go on for a while.

By February, most of the other candidates had dropped out of the race. The fight for the nomination was between Obama and Clinton.

Whoever the winner, it was a historic choice. It would be either the first female or first African-American presidential nominee from a major political party.

Obama and Clinton had similar opinions on most major issues. They both wanted to help middle-class and low-income Americans and broaden health care coverage.

They also had similar plans about the withdrawal of U.S. troops from Iraq.

Many voters supported Clinton. Her years of experience in Washington politics, both as first lady and senator, were impressive.

Obama, on the other hand, built his campaign around not being a Washington insider. He hadn't had much time to build a record in the senate or to make many unpopular votes.

Most importantly, voters saw him as new and fresh. He electrified audiences all over the country, projecting an image of youth and change.

17

Obama'08

BarackObama.com

SOLUTIONS FOR AMERICA

For the next few months, the two candidates were neck and neck. Obama would win one primary. Then Clinton would win another.

June 3, 2008

CHANGE WE CAN BELIEVE IN

But by early June, Obama finally won enough votes to be the Democratic nominee. That day, he and Michelle shared the most famous fist bump in history.

A few days later, Clinton officially ended her campaign.

I endorse him, and throw my full support behind him.

And I ask all of you to join me in working as hard for Barack Obama as you have for me.

People wondered if Clinton would be Obama's running mate. But Obama chose Senator Joe Biden of Delaware as the vice presidential nominee.

Biden was an expert in foreign affairs and had served the senate for 36 years.

CHAPTER 3

The General Election

The long campaign for the nomination was finally over. But the general election loomed. Now Obama had to go up against Republican John McCain, who had won his party's nomination in March.

McCain was a war hero. He was admired for his independent spirit and no-nonsense approach to issues. He was also 72 years old, making a 25-year age gap between him and Obama.

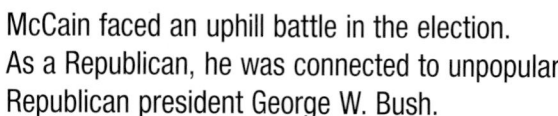

McCain faced an uphill battle in the election. As a Republican, he was connected to unpopular Republican president George W. Bush.

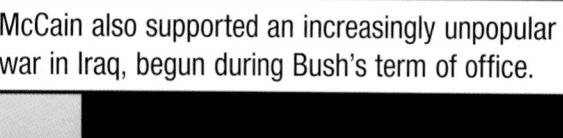

McCain also supported an increasingly unpopular war in Iraq, begun during Bush's term of office.

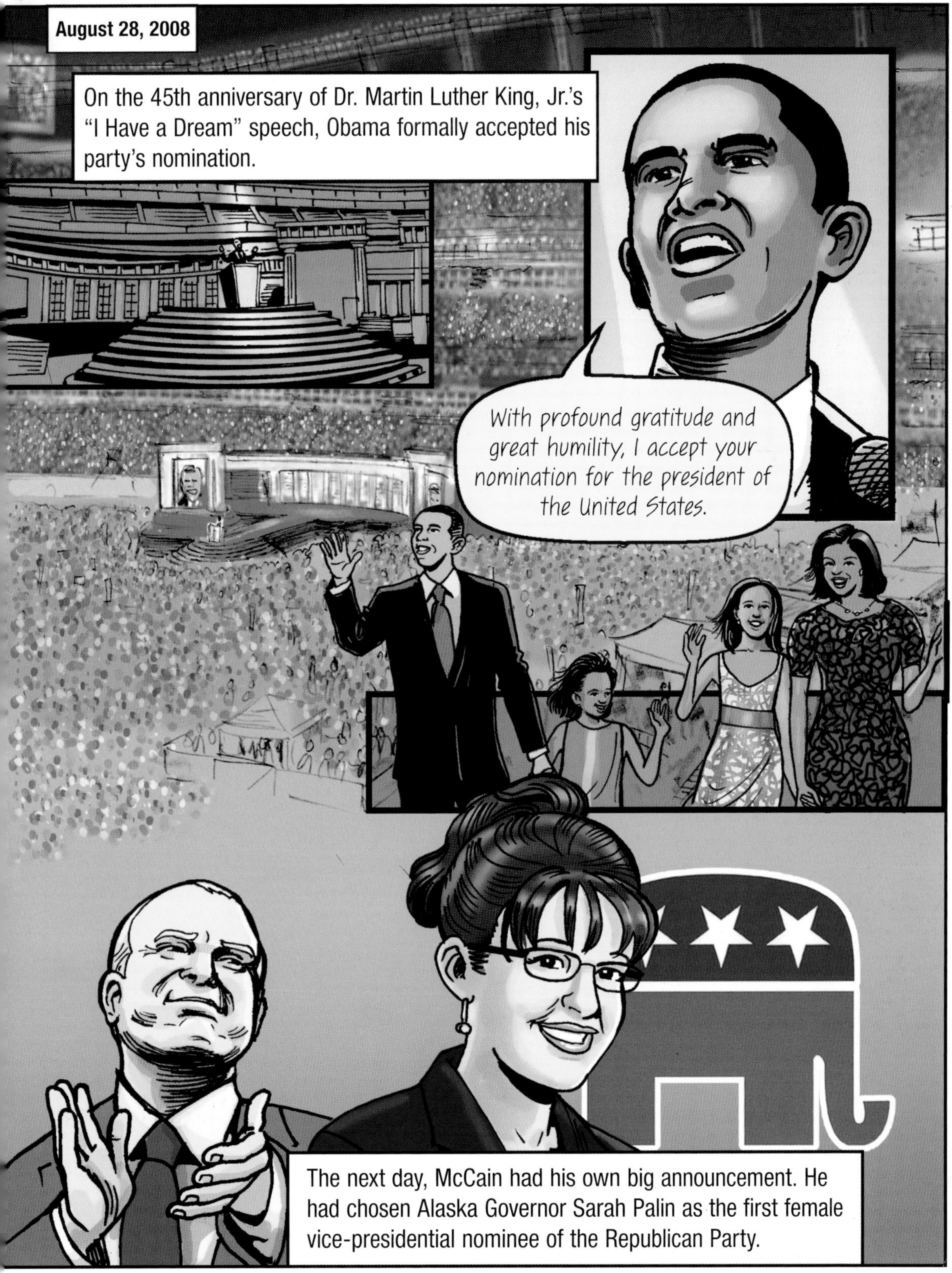
August 28, 2008
On the 45th anniversary of Dr. Martin Luther King, Jr.'s "I Have a Dream" speech, Obama formally accepted his party's nomination.
With profound gratitude and great humility, I accept your nomination for the president of the United States.
The next day, McCain had his own big announcement. He had chosen Alaska Governor Sarah Palin as the first female vice-presidential nominee of the Republican Party.

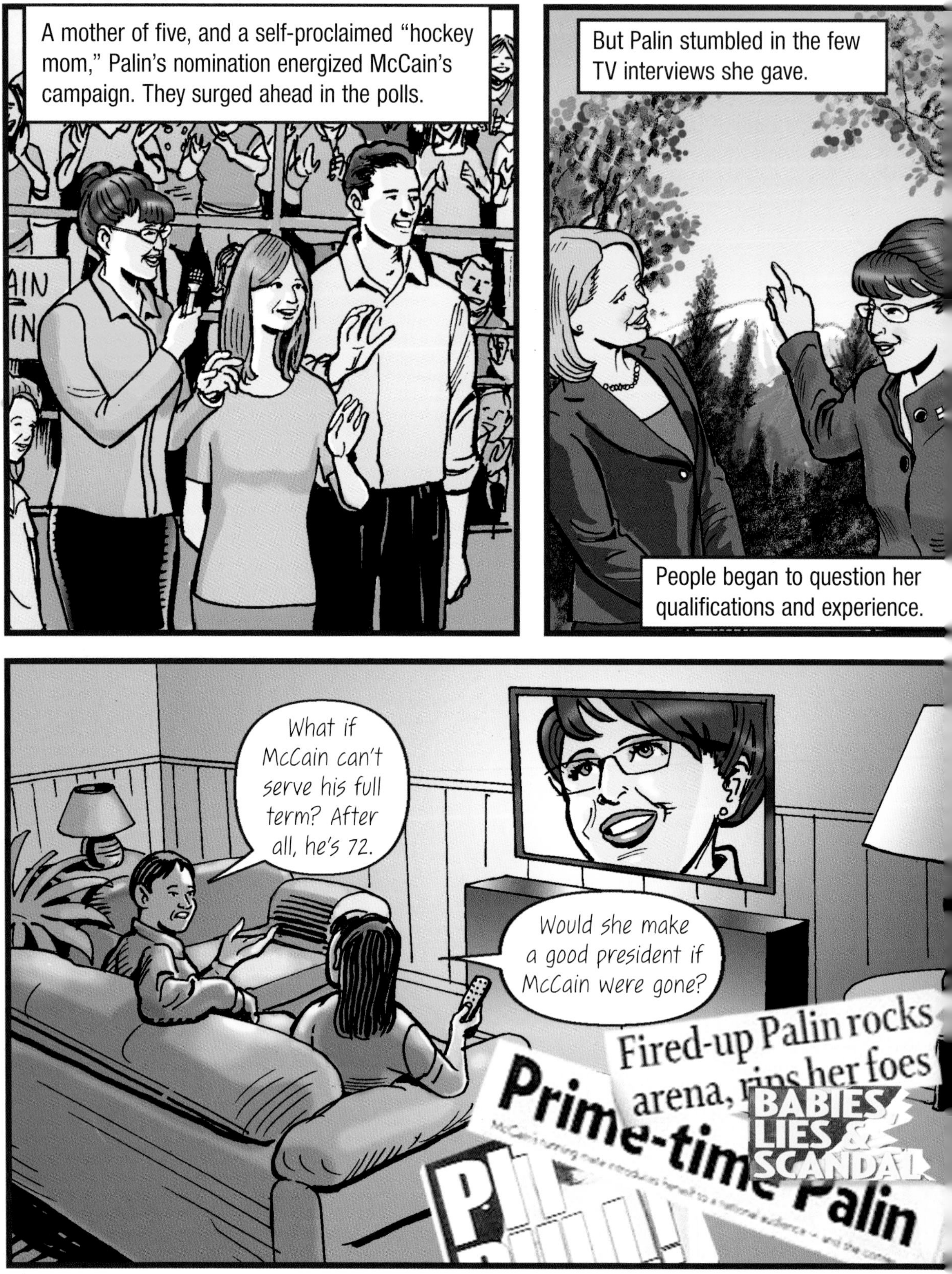
A mother of five, and a self-proclaimed "hockey mom," Palin's nomination energized McCain's campaign. They surged ahead in the polls.
But Palin stumbled in the few TV interviews she gave.
People began to question her qualifications and experience.
What if McCain can't serve his full term? After all, he's 72.
Would she make a good president if McCain were gone?
Fired-up Palin rocks
arena,
her foes
Prime-time Palin
BABIES, LIES & SCANDAL

About the same time, the U.S. economy fell apart. Huge industries neared collapse. Thousands of people lost their jobs every month. People saw their savings disappear. Others lost their homes.

LAYOFFS

FORECLOSED

The Gazette
HIGH UNEMPLOYMENT
JOBS SCARCE
NOTHING FOR GRADS

BUSINESS NEWS
FINANCIAL MELTDOWN

THE TIMES
CRASH OF 2008

September 15, 2008

Voters mostly blamed Republicans and their policies for the financial crisis. Speaking in Jacksonville, Florida, McCain tried to remain optimistic.

The fundamentals of our economy are strong.

Those words hurt McCain's campaign. People thought he didn't understand the seriousness of the situation.

Obama, on the other hand, was quick to say how serious the situation was.

I assure you, I am willing to take the steps necessary to correct the problems in our economy.

Obama and McCain had three televised debates.

McCain tried to present Obama as inexperienced. But Obama seemed calm and presidential when he spoke.

In polls about the debates, Obama came out a little better than McCain.

Obama had been leading in the polls for weeks, but he didn't want to take victory for granted.

Less than a week before Election Day, he bought 30 minutes of television time to promote his campaign.

It was a huge ratings success.

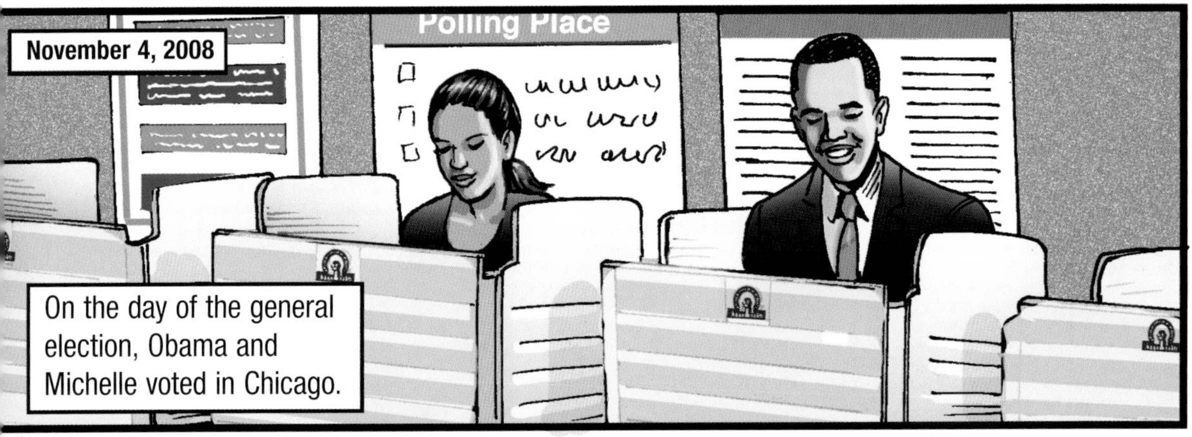

November 4, 2008
Polling Place
On the day of the general election, Obama and Michelle voted in Chicago.

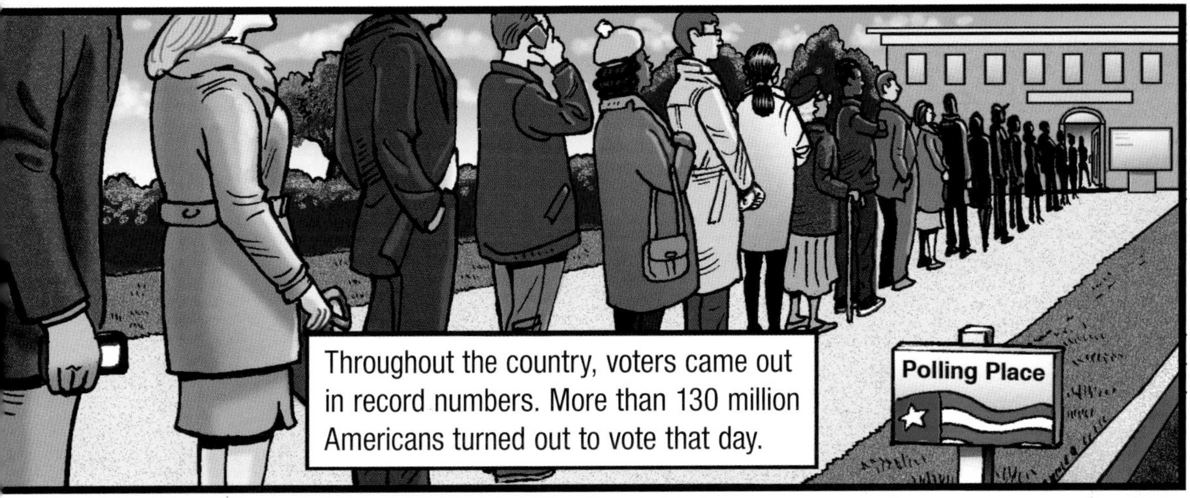

Throughout the country, voters came out in record numbers. More than 130 million Americans turned out to vote that day.
Polling Place

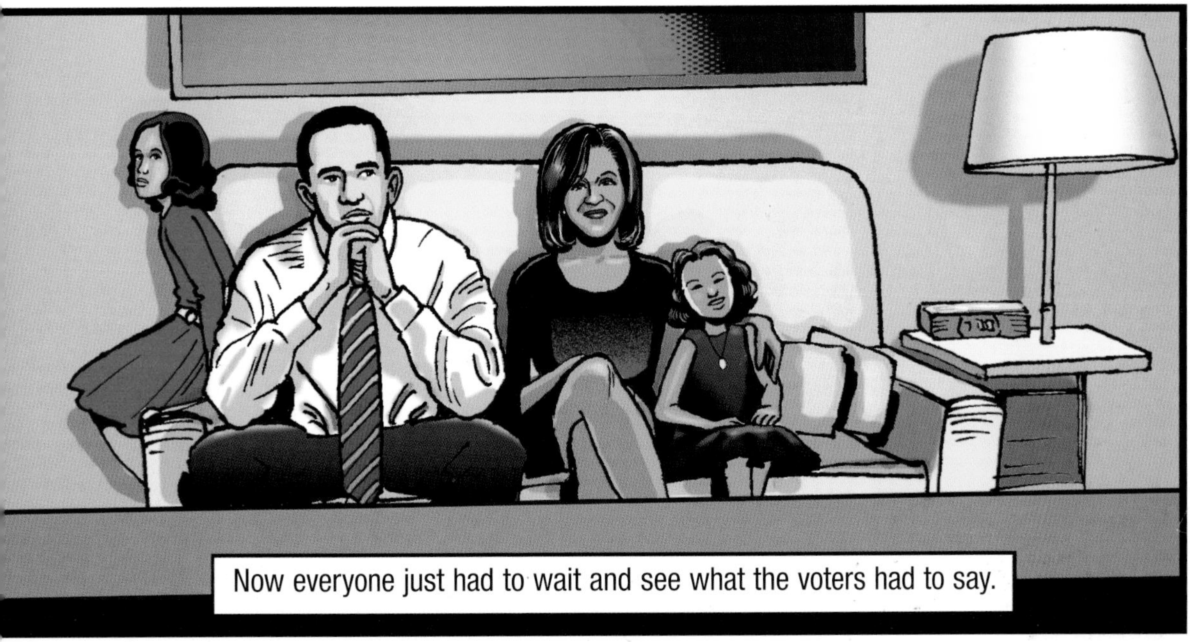

Now everyone just had to wait and see what the voters had to say.

Later that night, the news outlets declared a winner. The United States had elected its first African-American president. Obama received about 53 percent of the vote compared to about 46 percent for McCain.

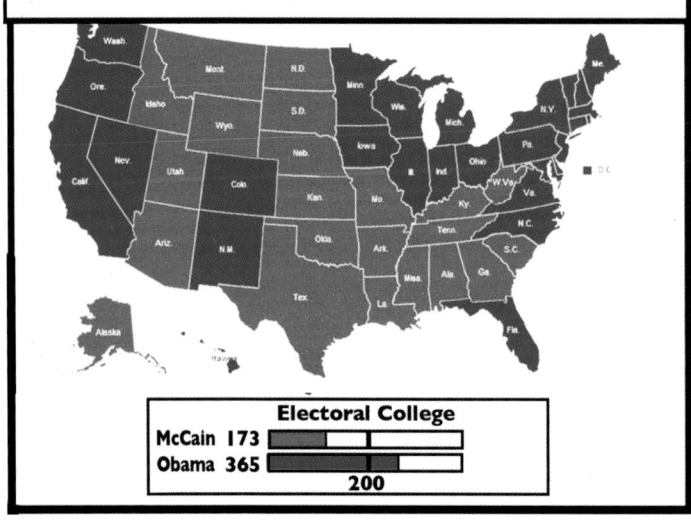

Electoral College

McCain 173		
Obama 365		
	200	

McCain conceded graciously.

This is a historic election, and I recognize the significance it has for African-Americans and for the special pride that must be theirs tonight.

After McCain's concession speech, Obama and his family went to Chicago's Grant Park to address the huge crowd waiting for them.

If there is anyone out there who still doubts that America is a place where all things are possible ...

YES WE DID!

... tonight is your answer.

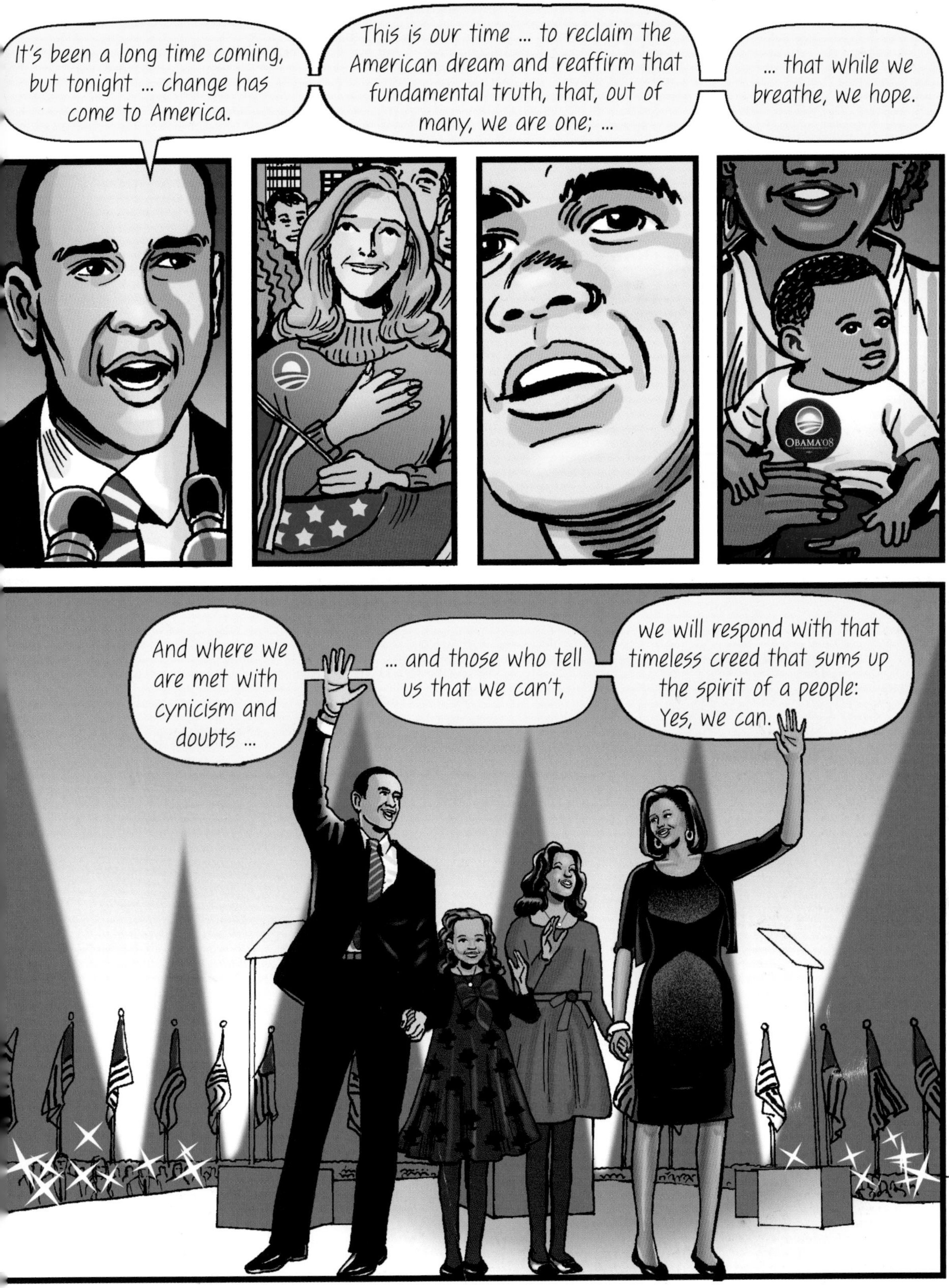
It's been a long time coming, but tonight ... change has come to America.
This is our time ... to reclaim the American dream and reaffirm that fundamental truth, that, out of many, we are one; ...
... that while we breathe, we hope.
OBAMA'08
And where we are met with cynicism and doubts ...
... and those who tell us that we can't,
we will respond with that timeless creed that sums up the spirit of a people: Yes, we can.

MORE ABOUT BARACK OBAMA

Barack Hussein Obama was born on August 4, 1961, in Honolulu, Hawaii. His mother was from Kansas and his father was from Kenya, a country in Africa. Barack's parents divorced when he was very young. His father returned to Africa.

His mother later remarried and the family moved to Jakarta, Indonesia, where Barack lived for four years. When Barack was 10 years old, he moved back with his grandparents in Hawaii so he could attend a better school.

In 1983 Barack graduated with a degree in political science from Columbia University in New York. He then moved to Chicago where he worked as a community organizer. He worked hard to help improve living conditions in poor African-American neighborhoods.

In 1988 Obama was accepted into Harvard Law School. He was the first African-American to be elected president of *The Harvard Law Review*, an honor that made national news. He graduated in 1991 and returned to Chicago. He worked as a civil rights lawyer and taught constitutional law at the University of Chicago. In 1992 he married attorney Michelle Robinson.

In 2008 Obama was elected the first African-American president of the United States. He was sworn in on January 20, 2009. At that time, the country was facing serious problems at home and abroad. The unemployment rate was very high, the economy was struggling, and there was an ongoing war in Iraq.

In February 2009 Obama signed into law a $787-billion economic stimulus package that was meant to shore up the economy. He promised that combat operations in Iraq would end by August 31, 2010. Obama also tried to repair the troubled relationship the U.S. had with the Muslim world.

In October 2009 Obama was awarded the Nobel Peace Prize. The prize honored him for his "extraordinary efforts to strengthen international diplomacy and cooperation between peoples." Then, in March 2010, Congress approved Obama's package of health care reforms. Obama felt these reforms would be his legacy to the nation.

candidacy (KAN-dih-duh-see)—the state or act of being a candidate; a candidate is someone who is applying for a job or running in an election

caucus (KAW-kuhs)—a gathering of people who elect delegates and discuss issues for party platforms

concede (kuhn-SEED)—to admit defeat in a contest or election

convention (kuhn-VEN-shuhn)—a large gathering of people who have the same interests, such as a political meeting where party candidates are chosen

front-runner (FRUHNT-RUHN-ur)—a leading contestant in a competition

keynote address (KEE-noht uh-DRESS)—a speech designed to present the issues of primary interest to an assembly

legislation (lej-uh-SLAY-shuhn)—laws that have been proposed or made

nominate (NOM-uh-nate)—to name someone as a candidate for an award, job, or government position

oath (OHTH)—a serious, formal promise

primary election (PRYE-mair-ee i-LEK-shuhn)—an election in which candidates of the same party try to win that party's nomination as candidate for a particular office

prominent (PROM-uh-nuhnt)—widely and popularly known

rival (RYE-vuhl)—a person or country competing with another for the same goal

tolerant (TOL-ur-uhnt)—willing to respect or accept the customs, beliefs, or opinions of others

READ MORE

Edwards, Roberta. *Who is Barack Obama?* New York: Grosset & Dunlap, 2010.

Hicks, Peter. *Barack Obama: President for Change.* Famous Lives. New York: PowerKids Press, 2011.

Krensky, Stephen. *Barack Obama.* DK Biography. New York: DK Pub., 2010.

Weatherford, Carole Boston. *Obama: Only in America.* New York: Marshall Cavendish, 2010.

INTERNET SITES

FactHound offers a safe, fun way to find Internet sites related to this book. All of the sites on FactHound have been researched by our staff.

Here's all you do: Visit *www.facthound.com*

Type in this code: 9781429660167

Check out projects, games and lots more at
www.capstonekids.com

AMERICAN GRAPHIC

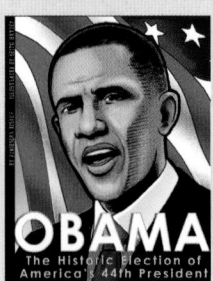

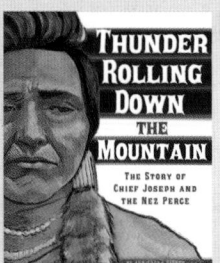